WHY I HATE ISRAEL

Why I Hate Israel: A Candid Account

ISBN 1-59689-004-5 (hardcover)
ISBN 1-59689-005-3 (paperback)

(USA) Library of Congress Control Number: 2004115623

Write-To Address:

The Hermit Kingdom Press
3741 Walnut Street, Suite 407
Philadelphia, PA 19104
United States of America

Info@TheHermitKingdomPress.com

★ ★ ★ ★

Hermit Kingdom
12 South Bridge, Suite 370
Edinburgh, EH1 1DD
Scotland

http://www.TheHermitKingdomPress.com

DEDICATED TO PALESTINIANS
AND OTHER OPPRESSED PEOPLES

Content

"Fear of death makes us devoid both of valor and religion. For want of valor is want of religious faith."

- Mahatma Gandhi

Why I Hate Israel

The Setting

Gosh, I hate Israel. There are many reasons why everyone should hate Israel. I can think of a million reasons.

I figured, why huff and puff in private. It's something that I can share. You can huff and puff along with me.

What is better, you can huff and puff and be informed at the same time. My purpose is to amuse you with information while sharing my pet-peeve.

See it this way. It's like eating sweet and sour sauce. How can sauce be both sweet and sour? It's either sweet or sour.

But the Chinese have pulled off the impossible. Sweet and sour sauce. It stems from the Chinese philosophy of ying and yang. Opposites can coexist in harmony.

In the same way, see my book as a way to have anger and entertainment exist in the same space.

You will be angry when you think about the colonialist, oppressive nature of Israel. But you will find yourself welling up with laughter as you see ironic humor in my writing.

You may find humor in all this. In fact, some say that the best way to survive oppression is through humor.

In essence, this book is a way of doing that. I am unabashedly condemning Israel and its oppression. I find myself in solidarity with the oppressed people.

Celebrating their humor and long-suffering, I would like to help them find humor as they resist evil and the oppression of Israel.

What is so evil about Israel? Israel is evil because it has a racist ideology. Zionism from the start was an ideology that was meant to be racist. And Zionism is still very alive. Some even try to force Zionism on the secular Israeli population which prefers a universalistic state benefiting all of the people living in the Land regardless of race or religion.

Another evil of Israel is its unabashed policy of oppression of Palestinians. It's hard to find humor in such a targeted policy backed by a powerful army. But if you are a helpless Palestinian Catholic being targeted, how will you deal with it? As civilians, humor may be just the ticket to get your family through the difficulty.

Thirdly, and perhaps related with the second point of official oppressive policy, Israel refuses to grant the Palestinians their independent state. There is nothing funny about being held in a limbo. You are not allowed to become a citizen of Israel and, thereby, you are excluded from the benefits of citizenship, and you are not allowed to have a state of your own, which will grant you citizenship and all the benefits pertaining to it. But I'll try to find vicarious humor in the midst of adversity.

Fourthly, Israel is a big bully in the region. Israel is always bragging that it has the best Air Force in the region. Israel regularly taunts its neighbors with tales about how it kicked the butts of all the nations that it wants peace with. Israel constantly calls its allies enemies. Israel brags about its nuclear arsenal. Israel is always depicting Arabic countries as inferior. There is much to poke fun of "Israel the Bully." And I will try my best not to restrain myself in lashing Israel with an intellectual whip.

I will focus on these areas throughout my book. I hope that this book of mine will be informative as well as entertaining.

I do not apologize for being socially conscientious. Perhaps, it is the result of being influenced by the proud tradition of Hindu support of the oppressed that propels my social consciousnesss. It may be the experience of India and Pakistan having being colonized for a long time that may be imbuing me with a social consciousness against colonialist oppression. It may be the fact that I find solidarity with women's rights movement that encourages me to speak out on social issues.

I am not sorry that various aspects of my experiences have raised social consciousness in me. And I am glad to continue to grow in my personal development and share my thoughts and experiences.

In the process, I hope that a greater awareness for the oppression in Israel will become visible on the global stage. I hope that there will be socially conscientious individuals rising all over the world who will not remain silent.

I choose the agency of candid writing as a way to share myself and my outlook with you. There are other ways to express support of human rights and civil justice. And I hope that there will be many readers out there who will fight against oppression represented in Israel in their own ways.

Zionism

Don't get me wrong. I don't think Zionism is all evil. Just because a group of people decide to call themselves a chosen race doesn't make them all evil.

Some of my closest friends are Zionists. And they do apologize before saying, "Yes, I believe that Jews are the race chosen by God."

It's a free country – at least, America is. Okay, Israel isn't so free. But it's free to express the idea that Jews are the chosen race in Israel. That idea is actually a privileged freedom of expression.

What I mean by that is that you are more free than free to say that Jews are the chosen race. In fact, it is the recommended freedom of speech.

The expression is so free that Members of the Parliament (which in Israel is called the Kenneset) officially emphasize the idea that Jews are the chosen race.

To the joy of all involved, particularly the secular Jews, religious Jews and also those who are gratuitously racist actually try to enact legislation to push policies that will exhibit this Jews-as-the-chosen-race principle.

Yep, what is the point of having an idea that Jews are the chosen race if you can't implement concrete measures to show the idea? It would be like saying ice cream is the best thing in the world and never eating it. It would be like thinking that plane is the greatest invention since ice cream and never flying. It would be like raving that planes with private movie screens with gazillion movies are a must when you travel and purposely avoiding planes with private screens in each seat because the ticket cost is 20 dollars more than a plane without. Yep, you get the idea!

It's like Nazism. What's the point of saying that Jews are the vermin of society, if you are not going to wipe out the Jews? It's like Jews who hate Hitler. What's the point of saying that Hitler is worse than a dog, if you don't take gratuitous pleasure in his downfall?

So, it seems goes the logic of Zionists who are super-duper-Zionists.

Jews are the chosen race. This has to account for something in policy. And dang-nash-nabit! Jews control Israel, so where better to implement this policy of the superiority of the Jews?

To the joy of neo-Zionists every-where, there are Kenneset members who will push and push to privilege the idea that Jews are the chosen race into policy.

Take for instance, Benny Alon. Yep, Mr. Alon is not alone, and Mr. Alon gladly hands out balon-ey! Now, if you like ba-loney, then you can have a mouthful. But if you are like me, I rather have my mouth baloney free, thank-you!

What's this baloney of Benny Alon? It's, of course, the kosher kind. Ultra ko-sher. More ultra kosher than there is word to describe it. And there is a good helping of Jews-are-the-chosen-race mustard sauce to go along with it.

Yep, that's what it is. Ultra kosher baloney. People like him are espousing an idea of a pure Jewish state. Just like a bunch of Presbyterians in a Christian School putting on *Fiddler on the Roof* seems so out of place, having non-Jews in the Jewish state is not quite right.

Just like having a vegan menu on Thanksgiving doesn't seem like a real Thanksgiving celebration, having Gentiles on the kosher homeland seems just so unkosher.

What would be the worst thing to do when you visit an Orthodox Jewish home? Bring ham as a welcome gift. Yep, ham is traditionally seen as a welcome-type gift, but it's just a big chunk of unkosher meat. You bring that stuff to an Orthodox Jewish household, not only do you offend them and may have them never speak to you again, but you may invariably defile their whole residence. Now, now, you wouldn't want to do that, would you. Wouldn't be prudent?

And in Benny Alon's book, so to speak, Gentiles are like the big chunk of ham dropped off on the doorstep of an Orthodox Jewish home.

What should you do with a big chunk of unkosher meat? Forgettaboutit! Well, actually not. They won't forget about it and just leave it there. There will be a swift process to discard the meat.

I feel like writing my address down right here and right now for any Orthodox Jew who may read this book and may be tempted to discard the unkosher meat.

You can send it to me! Yep, I am secular enough that I would take pleasure in consuming a big chunk of welcome-to-the-neighborhood ham. Yep, I would.

But how many Orthodox Jews will be reading this book? Really! With the title being what it is, I would be shocked if more than one Orthodox Jew read the book.

Don't they like read the Talmud all day and ignore the world, any way? At least, that's the picture that *The Chosen* seems to give about Orthodox Jews. They probably will not even know about the existence of this book. Yep, yep, yep. That's what it is.

And come to think about it. If they read this book, wouldn't they like get pissed off and take out a *fatwa* or some kind of death sentence against me and spread it around the circle of Orthodox Jews? Who knows? They may make some home-grown bombs and try to knock me off.

It happened with Prime Minister Itzak Rabin, and he was Jewish. An Orthodox Jew who was a law student at Bar Ilan University in Tel Aviv, Israel, shot Prime Minster Rabin dead at a 100% Jewish rally. I'm not Jewish, and I am not an Israeli

Prime Minister. I figure, it's probably easier to get a death sentence passed through the Orthodox Jewish synagogues and have some crazy Orthodox Jew hunting me down with a semi-automatic he purchased in the black-market of Brooklyn. Why give my address and make it easy for them to track me down. Yep, yep, yep.

So, throw your ham out. I wouldn't be able to eat a ham delivered to me anyway, if you did so after reading this book. You probably poisoned it.

Yep, if Orthodox Jews can gun down a Jewish Prime Minster in cold-blood, there are those capable of just about everything. Particularly against Gentiles.

And I assure you that no self-respecting Orthodox Jew will not throw away that ham. Yep, passing that ham to a secular Jew will go against their agenda to get all Jews to become Orthodox.

How about selling to Gentiles? Well, we are talking about one ham, right? You can't really open up shop with one piece of ham, can you?

How about selling it on e-bay? What if your Orthodox Jewish friends find out you are selling ham on e-bay? What are you going to tell them?

"Well, you see, I came across some ham and didn't want to let it go to waste, so I'm spending time and energy that I could spend on the Torah to watching wagering on the internet."

Well, I don't think so. It just wouldn't be prudent. And Orthodox Jews may be homicidal when it comes to Mr. Rabin, but they are no fool when it comes to matters of the Jewish Law.

Yep, it's safe to assume that the unkosher ham will be chucked out with a reckless abandon. Reckless abandon, I say.

And that's exactly what Benny Alon types want with Gentiles. Gentiles are like unkosher ham.

To give Mr. Alon some credit, we should acknowledge that Gentiles are unkosher. This is true. Most Gentiles will eat unkosher meat.

But then some Jews are unkosher, too. In fact, majority of English Jews are unkosher because they eat unkosher. So, what does this mean in the episode of "throw-out-the-welcome-ham"? More on that later. But for now, let's focus on the idea of Gentiles as unkosher ham. All right?

Yep, Gentiles are like unkosher ham. And the Alon faction wants unkosher ham thrown out. What does this mean in terms of legal policy? The Alon faction wants the Israeli Kenneset to pass laws to expel non-Jews.

Now, I hear you. You are probably saying, "Wha-a-a-t?" I hear ya. I hear ya loud an clear like the jet engine sound of an old plain flying dangerously low in Inglewood in Southern California. I hear ya like the gun shot sounds that is frequently heard in the streets of the Occupied Territories.

You are asking, "Haver, isn't that hypocritical?" Yep, I know. Jews are always complaining about how they were kicked out of countries for being Jewish, and now Jews want to kick non-Jews out?

Jews say non-Jews kicking Jews out is unethical but Jews kicking out non-Jews is ethical? And the Alon faction would say it was wrong for Gentiles to kick Jews out of Spain, England, and many other countries. But they'll say in the same breath that they should have a kicking-out policy (vis-à-vis the Gentiles) in Israel.

In one sense, you can say that this is a type of don't-get-screwed-but-screw-others-over ethics. Yep, that's what it is.

It's like a Jew saying it's wrong to deprive a Jew of an academic position just because he is Jewish and turning around and depriving an Arab of an academic position because he is an Arab.

It's like a Jew saying annihilation is wrong when it is done against Jews, but annihilation against non-Jews is okay.

What I am calling the Alon faction will certainly agree with this. The Alon faction is trying to push a policy to legalize driving out of all Arabs from Israel. The logic is that they can be absorbed by neighboring Arab countries.

Yep, the Alon faction believes that millions of Palestinians kicked out of Israel will find a home-sweet-home in other countries in the Middle East.

They speak as if all the Arabs are a homogenized whole and that all Arab nations have the same interest. It's like saying, Germany and France are exactly the same. It's like saying, kick people out of Russia, who can be identified as "European," and France and Germany should give them (even if in the millions) immediate citizenship.

It's like seeing all Arabs as the same. Yep, you hear this kind of rhetoric in other contexts. Most Europeans are familiar with the idea of "the Jew." Jews are perceived as a homogenized whole.

A Jew is a Jew. Jew in England is exactly the same as a Jew in France. Many Jewish intellectuals argue against such "objectifying" of Jews and homogenization. Jews in England are not the same as Jews in France.

The best way to see this is to get French Jews and English Jews in the same room and see what happens. They will be at each other's throats before the evening is over.

You can be sure of French Jews extolling the qualities of the French culture and English Jews getting offended because their English sensibilities have been ruffled.

French Jews will probably speak in French to each other and you'll have some English Jewish girl thinking how nice the

French accent is. And you will also have an English Jewish dude or two thinking how much they hate the French. English guys are always complaining about how the French are pretentious.

Yep, that's how it is. Jews in France are different from Jews in England. And why should they not be? Jews in France were enculturated in the French culture; Jews in England were brought up in English culture. It's only natural that they are products of their cultures.

Many liberal intellectual Jews have played the role of leaders fighting the objectification of Jews through homogenization.

Saying all Arabs are the same is just as ridiculous. Saying that Israel has the right to kick out Palestinians because there are Arab countries around is just asking for it.

World War 3, anyone? Sometimes, you wonder what's going through some people's minds. It may not matter if people doing such ridiculous thinking are some itinerant cynic philosopher, but when they are members of the Kenneset, you gasp in fear at the possible disaster ahead. Yep, that's exactly what it is. Gasp in fear.

Perhaps, you should hold your breath and hear this out. Not only does the Alon faction push for a type of expulsion hypothesis, it also supports the possibility of a genocide as a final solution.

In fact, you should not be surprised if the heroes of the Alon faction are Moses and Joshua, who happily carried out genocidal warfare.

Yep, the Alon factor does not rule out the possibility of a genocide of the Palestinians. It is true, however, that in terms of policy, it is the expulsion principle that is pushed.

Now, let us consider this. We are talking about a state that was founded on a principle that a people deserve their own state. The argument from Zionism is that Jews need a homeland to call their own. It was based on principles of self-determination.

But now, the Jews are turning around and saying that Palestinians must not have a Palestinian State? Israelis are saying that Palestinians do not have the right to self-determination while Jews do. Palestinians should be kicked around like a football in a rain-sodden field. This seems hardly fair.

Can the Israelis hold it against Arabs because they were born as Arabs and not as Jews? Should the Israelis induce a situation whereby every Arab child considers resenting the mother who gave birth to her? Why should Arabs be penalized for being Arabs in a land where they have lived for thousands of years.

It's like going into a new school and trying to institute the rule of your old school, when no one understands those rules.

Jews have lived outside of Palestine for the most of the past 2000 years and they entered into Palestine (Israel) only recently. The State of Israel is less than a hundred years old. So, it's like a new kid in the block coming in and trying to force the old kids in the block to abide by the rules.

It doesn't seem fair that a new people who came to take over the land as a result of colonialism are trying to kick out a people who have been living in the area for years and years and years. It's similar to the British kicking all the Chinese Hong Kong citizens out of Hong Kong and claiming that only British citizens should live in Hong Kong.

There seems to be a principle that those who lived in a land for a long time should have a claim to it. In fact, this is, to a certain extent, a foundation of western property law.

Kicking all the non-Jews out of Israel does not seem to be a viable policy or an ethical policy.

You would think that Jews learned their lessons regarding genocide and mass expulsion from their own experiences. But apparently not.

Ironically, measures that some Jews perceive as protecting Jews are actually the precise measures that endanger all Jews. The fact that the Israeli Kenneset allows this kind of idea is an encouragement to the rest of world to have neo-Nazi elements in their governments. In a global community that we live in, with internet providing ready access to information and news, Israel cannot really condemn neo-Nazi elements in French and German governments, let's say, as Israel allows the Alon faction in the Israeli government.

In other words, what the Israeli government is doing in Israel gives the needed incentive and rationale for European governments to go neo-Nazi (or in that direction).

Israelis must assume that Europeans are not stupid. Jews must not assume that Europeans are ignoring what is going on in Israeli government proceedings, which are being tracked by media, both left and right.

There are a lot of intellectuals and powerful people in European governments who have a hatred of Jews. The Jew-hatred may rise as a part of social conditioning based on 2000 years of European history or because of personal experiences. Whatever may be the factor, it is safe to assume that there are many individuals who privately hate Jews in Europe.

What Israel does in terms of allowing anti-Arab, anti-Muslim policies (including almost genocidal ones) even on an official government level can and will give others the rationale (ethical, moral, and intellectual) to push ahead with ant-Jewish policies.

It's not surprising that European governments recently have been going in the direction of neo-Nazis. There are certainly neo-Nazis from Herder to Le Pan who have gained massive public support in different European countries on a political, governmental level.

What Israel is doing is endangering the lives of all Jews in Europe in the long run. The State of Israel, through their extremist Zionism, is providing an example of exclusivism that will justify exclusivism of Jews in Europe on an official level in the modern world.

Yep, that's what it is. You have to be stupid not to know that such a pro-Zionist ideology and governmental policy in Israel are well-witnessed and documented by intellectual and policy. It's a matter of record open for everyone around the world, from intellectuals to casual web-surfers, to access.

Some may find it ironic that it is Zionism that endangers the lives of Jews, particularly in Europe. Wasn't Zionism supposed to save the Jews, some may ask?

But let's face it. Did European Jews benefit from Zionism in any real way? Not really. Some say that without the rise of exclusive Zionism in Germany from 1840s to 1910s, there would not have been a targeted genocide of Jews.

Zionism was an aggressive rejection of all non-Jews, and non-Jews resented Jews for it. Zionism was published in print, expounded in social circles, and pushed in front of Gentile faces.

How is this the case? Consider for the historically relevant but fictional example of a German Jew who is aggressively Zionist. We will call him Joe-Schmo-Zionist.

Here is this Joe-Schmo-Zionist living in Germany. He was born in Berlin, his father was born in Berlin, and his grandfather was born in Berlin. In fact, as far as his family is aware, they have always lived in Berlin.

The family line had been religiously Jewish, by in large. In the 1800s, when many Orthodox Jews in Germany were becoming modern Orthodox influenced by Moses Mendelssohn, Joe-Schmo-Zionist's grandfather became modern Orthodox. Then, his son, Joe-Schmo-Zionist's father, became secular. Joe-Schmo-Zionist grew up in a secular Jewish home that occasionally attended a Reformed Jewish synagogue in Berlin.

Joe-Schmo-Zionist is completely secular, does not believe in God, does not keep kosher, is dating non-Jewish women, and is attending the Humboldt University as a law student.

Joe-Schmo-Zionist, in fact, despises all things that are traditionally associated with Orthodox Judaism and identified with the Jewish Ghetto. Most of Joe-Schmo-Zionist's friends are non-Jewish.

While studying in Berlin, Joe-Schmo-Zionist is exposed to the ideas of Solomon Schlechter and other Zionists. Joe-Schmo-Zionist embraces Zionism and starts to emphasize the principles of Zionism.

Joe-Schmo-Zionist argues that Jews are Jews and that that must be the primary identity of all Jews, whether religious or not. Joe-Schmo-Zionist is swept away in the exclusive rhetoric of Zionism and starts arguing that German Jews are not really German, but that they are Jews, first and foremost.

Joe-Schmo-Zionist starts a local newspaper devoted to Zionism and a discussion group for Zionist ideas.

Joe-Schmo-Zionist starts to publish articles arguing that it's important for Jews to recognize their Jewish identity. Joe-Schmo-Zionist writes that Jews in Germany who do not extol their Jewish identity over their German identity are fooling themselves. He writes further that Jews must not see themselves as German or see their German identity as superior to their Jewish identity.

Joe-Schmo-Zionist writes that Jews belong to a separate nation. Jews are all, by the virtue of the fact that they are Jews, belonging to the Jewish nation. He argues that all Jews must be aware of their membership in the Jewish nation and that they must push to privilege the Jewish nation over all other national loyalties.

Joe-Schmo-Zionist argues that a German Jew must be loyal to the Jewish nation and not to the German nation. Joe-Schmo-Zionist passes around *The Jewish State by* Theodor Herzl in his Zionist discussion groups.

At first, his Gentile German friends think that it's a phase that Joe-Schmo-Zionist is going through. With the passage of time, it becomes clear that Joe-Schmo-Zionist is not going through a phase. His Gentile German friends begin to read his writings on Zionism as spare copies of his newspapers lie around the Humboldt University.

Joe-Schmo-Zionist's friends are shocked by the idea that he is more loyal to a Jewish nation than to the German nation. His friends are personally offended by Joe-Schmo-Zionist's apparent rejection of German culture and tradition. His friends have never seen him as anything more than German, but after reading his writings, his Gentile friends doubt his Germanness.

Being interested in what Joe-Schmo-Zionist is writing, his Gentile friends read more and more of what is being written from the Zionist perspective. The Gentile German friends become increasingly offended at the us-versus-them rhetoric that they see in Zionism.

Some begin to say, "He really dislikes Germans, doesn't he?" At first, some Gentile German friends try to defend Joe-Schmo-Zionist, but with the passage of time, they are finding that they are increasingly in the minority. More and more of Joe-Schmo-Zionist's Gentile friends are being offended by Zionist principles, primarily because they see them as a rejection of Germany and the Gentile world.

Even liberal-minded Gentiles who like Jewish religious literature and tried to incorporate them in thinking about ethics become offended at the exclusive nature of Zionism. Gentile Germans feel that they are being accused, but they feel that they have done nothing wrong. They feel like they were being accused of something unjustly and they start to see Zionism in a very negative light.

More and more of Joe-Schmo-Zionist's Gentile friends reject Zionism and its claims. They become personally offended that Joe-Schmo-Zionist is loyal to an exclusive ideology that is anti-German. Some Germans start to use the word, "racist," to describe Zionism because it pictures the Jewish nation in race terms and excludes the German race, explicitly.

Joe-Schmo-Zionist's Gentile friends feel that they are being intellectually cornered and feel a need to retaliate against Zionism and its exclusive claims, phrased against Germans and Germany.

German nationalism begin to exhibit itself on campus. Liberal Gentile Germans catch the sight of a flier about German nationhood. They might have thrown the flyer away in the past, but after their experience with Zionism and Joe-Schmo-Zionist, they attend the initial meeting out of curiosity. German nationalist meetings seem to say the same things that Zionism says, but it does not reject Germans or the German identity. Gentile friends of Joe-Schmo-Zionist continue to attend the meetings of German nationalism and read more literature on the issue. They feel that the rejection they experienced from Joe-Schmo-Zionist and Zionism is comforted by their participation in the German nationalist discourse. Some of them become active supporters of German nationalism and others become passive (but tacitly sup-portive) agents of emerging German nationalism. And some of them actually join newly formed political organizations dedicated to German nationalism.

It is the rejection perceived to be inherent in Zionism that propelled many of Joe-Schmo-Zionist's friends to the other end. They felt personally humiliated and rejected. Going the other way was the way to assuage their personal sense of insult and anger.

This scenario was more widely spread that people tend to give credit for. Zionism might have fuelled Jewish identity among Jews, but it was not done in a vacuum. Zionist writings were written in local languages and were readily accessible to both Jews and non-Jews. Anyone could read it in the same way information about Israel and Israeli policies are readily available in the internet for the global community, today.

No one likes rejection. Gentile Germans rejected by Zionism and Joe-Schmo-Zionist did not like the rejection either.

Perhaps, an example is in order to illustrate the powerful phenomena of rejection. Let's suppose you are living in Philadelphia. The local football team is the Philadelphia Eagles.

The week before the Superbowl, everyone in Philadelphia is excited. Everybody in your school is wearing Eagles clothing. Everyone is talking about Eagles and the victory that they want for their home team.

You show up in school wearing the shirt of the opposing side and say that you want them to win because your father lives there and you used to go and watch football games with him and support the team when you were younger.

What people will hear is not that you are celebrating your childhood memories and your childhood loyalties. What people in your school will hear is that you oppose the Philadelphia Eagles. People in your school will resent the fact that you are not loyal to the Philadelphia Eagles, which is the local team, but rather you are dedicated to the other team. The fact that many actually hate the other team by the virtue of the fact that your local team is playing against them will certainly not endear you to them.

Most likely, you will be hated by your classmates because you are supporting the "enemy" team. The other team, were it not playing against your team, may not be hated so much. In fact, what the other team is does not really matter. The fact that you are not supporting the Philadelphia Eagles, the local team, is the real issue.

This example explains the phenomena of Zionism in the German context. When Jews were saying that Jews were not really German, it was rejecting Germans. It might not have mattered what they were rejecting Germany with. The fact was that Zionists were defining Jews against Germany and that was problematic in the eyes of many Germans.

Germans saw Zionism not so much as an affirmation of Jewish identity as a rejection of Germans. It is like you not supporting the Philadelphia Eagles. You may have the best reasons for supporting the other team, but the reasons will fall on deaf ears.

Just like people's resentment in the Philadelphia Eagles' case can erupt into violence, Zionism's alienation of Germans anticipated the possibility of violence.

The German case is not unique. Although Zionism is identified as a particular ideology at a particular time in history, there have been tendencies to identify a central Jewish identity for the Jewish communities. Ancient Romans, for instance, complained of Jews isolating themselves in the Roman Empire. At the height of prosperity for Jews in Alexandria, Jews encountered massive violence. Many explain the violence as resulting from the perception in the Roman Empire that the Jews were rejecting them through their elevation of Jewish group identity.

There have been other examples of Jewish centralization that resulted in the general perception in the larger society that they were rejecting them. Particularly in modern history, there have been quite a number of examples of expulsions, pogroms, and genocide against Jews.

Of course, gratuitous violence is not justifiable. However, they must not be ignored. Something can be learned from them. More often than not, these cases are explainable by the Rejection Factor.

History is useful because you can learn from it. You can learn and ensure that same tragedy does not befall you. Jews will do well to learn from the mistakes of Zionism. Zionism should be seen as at least a major contributing factor to the Holocaust.

It is unwise for the modern secular state of Israel to continue a discourse of Zionism. It is not useful in the current international climate. It hurts Israel's image and alienates countries that might otherwise support Israel and Jews.

And it is not like all religious Jews like Zionism. Many Orthodox Jews resent Zionism, which was a secular ideology of Jewish nationalism at the start. Orthodox Jews want the Messiah to inaugurate the New Age, not a bunch of pork-eating, secular Zionists. There are, certainly, fundamentalist Orthodox Jews who have come to incorporate Zionism in their system. The Alon Faction is certainly a good example. But certainly there are Orthodox Jews who oppose the concept of a secular Jewish state.

Zionism is, indeed, a loose-loose proposition. But it does not seem like Israel is changing its course. Israel seems to uphold the ideology of Zionism. Given its unethical nature, I would certainly have to say it is one of the major reasons why I hate Israel. Not only is Zionism unethical and racist, it highlights the stupidity and the backwardness of the Jewish State that refuses to enter the pluralistic modernity.

Oppression

Oppression is an evil thing. There is hardly anyone in the world who would disagree with that. Maybe if you are Sadam Hussein, you may try to argue that oppression is a good thing. The only country that purports to be democratic but has a systematic program of oppression (without shame) is the State of Israel.

The State of Israel has elevated the oppression of Palestinians to an art form. Israel oppresses Palestinian Catholics and Muslims (two largest religious groups among Palestinians) so much that the Vatican has taken an official stance against the State of Israel. The Vatican's anti-Israel stance in regards to the oppression of Palestinians is an ethical stance.

The Roman Catholic Church has an obligation to the Kingdom of Christ and the vicar of the Kingdom on earth, the Pope, has an obligation to look out for the members of the Body of Christ, so goes the Catholic discourse. As a significant number of the Palestinians being affected are Roman Catholics, the Vatican has the ethical obligation to make a visible and audible stance. And to the credit of the Vatican, the ethical stance has been proactively taken.

Where are all these Christians, you may ask? There are pockets of Palestinian Christians throughout the Occupied Territories. The most visible resistance comes from Ramallah. At least half of Ramallah's population is thought to be Roman Catholic. And those who are aware of the history of the *intifada* will know that Ramallah is like the Irish Belfast.

Many Palestinian Catholics provided the brain-power and the logistic support to resistance programs and other forms of active protests. More often than not, these protests were not terrorist activities although the State of Israel tried to paint them as such. The demonstrations tended to be group marches with children occasionally throwing stones at the Israeli police.

Although demonstrations often tended to be peaceful than not, there were, to be sure, Roman Catholics, who involved themselves in a more militant (even violent) resistance against what they perceived as unjust oppression. Violent resistance to perceived oppression is nothing new in the Christian community. Irish Catholics have long engaged in conscientious protests by peaceful and militant means against what they perceived to be unjust oppression.

The Anglican tradition encourages acting according to conscience and allows even violent resistance against injustice. Baptist and Presbyterian traditions have many examples of resistance against what they perceived as unjust oppression, and many theologians in the two denominations have actively upheld the principle of the right to use violence to fight unjust oppression. The Roman Catholic Church has many other examples of violent resistance to perceived unjust oppression. Practical examples are found in South America with much theological writing stemming from experience in the form of Liberation Theology.

Christianity from the very beginning recognized the need to resist injustice. There has always been a tacit understanding that violent resistance to alleviate unfair suffering and unjust oppression was not only acceptable but necessary. The image of Jesus Christ coming back in glory and splendor with his heavenly armies conjure up images of violent resistance to injustice.

Most Hindus have found Gandhi's ideas of non-violent resistance very attractive. But many Hindus, particularly recent intellectuals, have politely disavowed Gandhi's ideas as being variable in the present world. A part of the reason for a move away from peaceful resistance is due to practical and historical considerations. The problem of Kashmir and conflict with Pakistan has shown Hindus that militant and violent resistance is necessary. Hindus did not, by in large, object to the developing of nuclear bombs capable of killing millions of civilians in a blink of an eye. Gandhi's fundamental philosophical stance would condemn such a weapon of mass destruction.

But to be honest, Hinduism has never been as "peaceful" as Gandhi tried to make it out to be. Even in his day, many Hindus disagreed with his principles of non-violent resistance, even though they respected his personal efforts and his charisma. More so today, Hindus have all but completely pushed aside Gandhi's fundamental tenets.

In fact, the past few decades have seen the rise of Hindu fundamentalism. Some secular tending Hindus have openly condemned the trend. But to think that Hindu Fundamentalism is an ignorant movement is to miss the reality of the situation.

Many of the leaders of Hindu Fundamentalism are very educated. Hindu Fundamentalism is discoursed in intellectual terms, even employing some of the most recent philosophical concepts.

Some see Hindu Fundamentalism as a reaction to Muslim Fundamentalism, but this is too simplistic. Although Muslim Fundamentalism may have given an impetus to Hindu Fundamentalism, Hindu Fundamentalism should be seen as a diachronic development with a synchronic discourse. Seen positively, Hindu Fundamentalism is an effort to protect Hinduism and Hindus. It can be seen as a defensive mechanism with a positive goal. It can also be argued that Hindu Fundamentalism fundamentally stands in opposition to any kind of unjust aggression to Hinduism and Hindus.

As a secular Hindu, I do not necessarily buy into Hindu Fundamentalism. But even leftist Hindu as I must concur that the intentions are more pure than not. I laud the fundamental idea that unjust oppression must be resisted. And although I do not espouse unnecessary violence, I recognize the fact that violent resistance may, indeed, become necessary. As the saying goes, even a mouse which is cornered by a cat will fight the cat, there are instances in which only violent resistance becomes the only way to fight unjust oppression.

Thus, Hinduism in essence agrees with Christianity in the emphasis on resisting unjust oppression. Just as the Vatican condemns Israeli oppression, most Hindus would condemn Israeli oppression of Palestinians.

In other words, resistance offered by Ramallah Catholics would be considered ethical both in the Catholic religion and in the Hindu religion.

And Ramallah is not the only place where Roman Catholics are found. There is a significant Roman Catholic population in Bethlehem. Some say that over 50% of the city is Roman Catholic. Although Bethlehem tended not to be as visible in its resistance against Israeli oppression, in spirit they have upheld the idea of resistance against unjust oppression.

Roman Catholics have played prominent roles in structuring resistance in the Occupied Territories. And Palestinians have been assisted by well-meaning Catholics from other countries who have come to settle in the area.

The fact is that Jerusalem is a very holy city for Christians. There is a reason why the Crusades were started with Christians as far away as England travelling on foot to make Jerusalem a Christian city. Because of the value that Jerusalem has in Christian traditions, Christians are more actively involved in the area than generally assumed. There are both laity and clergy attached to Christian holy sites, like the Church of the Nativity in Bethlehem, and they seek to provide Christian education and identity to the church-goers.

Many Christian leaders came to identify with the suffering of the masses and more than a few protest either directly or indirectly against Israeli oppression. Even if Christian individuals do not resist against the Israeli government directly, they provide a form of indirect protest in getting the information (including concrete real-life examples) of Israeli oppression out to the folks back home. Slowly information spreads and more and more people who identify themselves as Christians participate in sympathy or empathy on behalf of the oppressed.

And, certainly, it would not be a surprise to find a causal link between the presence of Christians in the Occupied Territories and nearby areas and the resolutions in the United Nations officially condemning the State of Israel through multi-national votes.

Christian organizations, like the Vatican, issue official condemnations based on reliable testimonies and evidence. In other words, there is a lot of documentable evidence that supports institutional condemnation of the State of Israel's oppression of Palestinians.

Indeed, the oppression of Palestinians is a well-known fact. The state of Israel has distinguished itself as the oppressor in several ways.

First of all, the State of Israel oppresses the Palestinians by closing down the borders (between Israel proper and the Occupied Territories) periodically. To be fair, there are times when the State of Israel has legitimate reasons to close down the borders. If there is uncontrollable conflict between the demonstrators (no matter how just the cause) and a defensive force, Israeli authorities may want to close down the borders between the Occupied Territories and the State of Israel proper to defend the civilian population.

However, the problem is that more often than not, the State of Israel closes down the borders as a type of control mechanism to display its power and remind the Palestinians of their oppressed status. In a very real way, closing down the borders is a type of psychological oppression of the Palestinian people.

But border closures are not merely psychological. There are real consequences to border closures. Besides the humiliation, there is the practical problem of restriction to travel. Given the fact that the Occupied Territories are divided into several regions, border closures mean that Palestinians cannot travel to other parts of the Occupied Territories. (For example, travel to Gaza from Ramallah requires going through Israel proper.) This means that Palestinians are not able to visit relatives in other parts of the Occupied Territories.

But border closures mean more than social restrictions. Palestinians living in the Occupied Territories often work in other parts of the Occupied Territories, and border closure means that they will not be able to go to work. And some Palestinians hold jobs in Israel itself, and they too cannot enter their place of work when the borders are closed.

Given that border closures tend to be quite frequent and sometimes last for many days, the loss of wages can be debilitating personally. Some families are, in fact, cast into poverty and actual hunger as the direct result of border closures.

The fact that border closures by the Israeli government is done as a matter of policy control more than anything else, human rights activists and agencies find the whole situation appalling. Many perceive border closures as a type of "whipping" or slavery.

But the oppressive measure draws complaints not only from the Palestinian side and objective third parties. Some Israelis are affected by border closures as well. Israelis who employ Palestinians may suffer loss of productivity. However, the population of Israeli businesses which suffers as the result of border closures is small in number as to be insignificant.

Perhaps, that is the reason why border closure policies are not being changed. If more Israeli businesses suffer directly as the result of border closures, more would be done to change policies.

In fact, we must note that there are those who actually benefit from border closures. Although not many Israelis venture into the Occupied Territories, there are Israelis who make the journey in search of bargains in shopping. Products and food are generally much cheaper in the Occupied Territories and parts of them are a mere 30 minute bus ride away from Jerusalem.

Palestinian businesses, therefore, take customers away from Israeli shops and businesses. Sporadic and frequent border closures tend to discourage Israelis from forming the habit of bargain shopping in the Occupied Territories. And this suits Israeli big businesses just fine as they are situated for large profit taking from the Israeli population.

It is clear that border closures benefit Israeli businesses more than not and thus there is a type of economic support on the Israeli side for border closures. Political control is, therefore, a type of economic control to restrict free market and *laissez-faire* competition that may detract from Israeli corporate profits.

Economic advantage coupled with political expediency fuels continued policy of border closings as intentional oppressive policy on the Occupied Territories. Obviously, the political situation being what it is, the Occupied Territories cannot respond fairly in defence.

And Palestinians suffer. Individuals, families, and businesses in the Occupied Territories are effectively stunted in their growth and development. The oppressive policy has impoverished many families and individuals.

Many concerned with fair play and human rights are voicing their disgust at the official oppressive policy more and more. As there are implications in human rights law and international (corporate) law, the European Union and other international bodies are being more critical of the practices, such as border closing in Israel.

Certainly, border closing is not the only oppressive policy of Israel, although it may be the best known, most practiced, and generally the most far-reaching. Israeli government has proven itself to be a great oppressor in its periodic bulldozing of Palestinian houses as well.

Yep, you have heard it right. The Israeli government engages in a periodic bulldozing of Palestinian houses. The excuse, of course, is that they are targeting evil terrorists.

But come on! Do you think that going around and completely destroying people's homes is a constructive way to stop terrorism?

And the fact is that most of the bulldozing is of civilian homes. Israelis do not know where terrorist homes are, so they retaliate against the civilian population.

Now, think about this. If there are terrorists in the fringe of society and you go around bulldozing normal people's houses, naming the supposed terrorists as the reason, what will happen? Is it not possible that you will created unwanted sympathy and support for the terrorists by the people, whose homes have been bulldozed?

And let's not forget. These people have relatives, friends, and neighbors. Is it any wonder that Israel doesn't seem to be making friends with its supposed enemies (or generated enemies)?

Americans, to their credit, have been quite smart about things. You don't see Americans in Iraq going indiscriminately among the civilian population and bulldozing their houses every time things blow up and American soldiers die.

Americans are concerned about winning the good will of the Iraqi people. And despite all their faults, Americans actually try to accomplish their civilian-friendly objectives.

Furthermore, Americans have a fundamental respect for private property. American respect for other people's property is clearly visible in American laws.

The American system fundamentally respects people's right to private property. In fact, most Americans believe that one of the most important functions of the government and the police is to protect private property.

Americans have not failed to assert this policy in Iraq and in other areas that they have conquered in wars. It was that way in Japan and in Germany after World War 2. Americans have a fundamental respect for private property, even if it is the private property of civilians in enemy lands.

Israelis certainly do not subscribe to the American model. Bulldozing civilians' private houses show fundamental disrespect for private property. Yep, that's what it is.

Israel certainly is not America.

It should be pointed out that protecting private property is more than respecting other people's property. In America and Western Europe, the concept of property is tied to the concept of a person. In fact, in legal terms, property is seen as an extension of the self.

Your private property is a part of who you are. This legal understanding of property is understandable in light of the function of property in America and Western Europe.

The home you own profiles you in a certain way. In order to get credit (which in fact is a way to assess your worth as someone creditable), institutions try to ascertain the extent and worth of your property.

Often, the house you live in is perceived to determine your credit-worthiness as a person. Your house, thus, allows you to borrow money from banks for college education, business ventures, medical expenses, and other types of financial support available in the economic system.

The fact that the Israeli government indiscriminately bulldozes Palestinian civilian homes as a type of colonialist control mechanism shows that Israel not only does not respect people's private property but they also do not respect the personhood of the individuals affected by bulldozing.

It is important to emphasize that home insurance does not cover government bulldozing your house. This is the case in Palestine as well as in the USA. In America, this would not happen, of course. There is ample ways to retaliate against the government – legally, politically, socially, etc. – if the American government were to turn its back on the fundamental American respect for private property and started to bulldoze people's houses indiscriminately.

Yep, Israel is no America.

You can see why I dislike Israel. Israel is an oppressive bully that has no respect for civilians. Israel has no respect for people.

In fact, bulldozing civilian homes clearly shows that Israelis think of Palestinians as less than human. There is an innate racist outlook that is simply disgusting. No self-respecting citizen of the world in the 21st Century should tolerate this kind of racist behavior from the State of Israel.

And the State of Israel has to recognize that bulldozing homes is a stupid thing to do. Don't the Jewish leaders know western history and the history of private property? Do Israelis think that such a behavior will go unnoticed in the Internet Age?

Bulldozing homes is fundamentally stupid because it pictures Israel as an ethically evil nation. It's not like the Jewish State conjures up warm and fuzzy feelings in the minds of most people in the world. Bulldozing just adds to the dislike.

Who can like a nation that indiscriminately bulldozes people's private property?

Would you like your property bulldozed on a whim of a government? People can feel empathetic sympathy for those who experience any form of violation of their private property. Americans have a saying: "A man's home is his castle."

Yep, you don't just go and raze someone's castle. It is tantamount to a declaration of war.

Besides border blocks and bulldozing, Israel is prominent in another form of oppression. It is what I like to call, "keeping people down policy."

Israel tries to keep Palestinians down by oppressive measures that prevent the creation of better educational institutions and social agencies that can help people.

"Keeping people down policy" can be seen as a form of oppression because it is denial of rights and advantages that people can have if it were not for an active policy to oppress people.

"Keeping people down policy" can be seen particularly in the area of education. The Israeli government works hard to ensure that educational levels in the Occupied Territories do not find much advancement.

Most visibly, this is done in the form of withholding of funds from major universities in the Occupied Territories where Palestinians go to study. The idea is that if there is a lack of funds, there will not be enough money to provide for a good education, resulting in over all educational deprivation of the population. Deprivation of good education, thus, can be seen as a policy to maintain effective oppression.

If you can do all you can to block possible leaders from emerging, you can keep the people subjugated.

Of course, what Israel fails to realize is that having good, conscientious, intelligent leaders could actually work in their favor in the long-run. Without capable leaders, good negotiation and cooperation is difficult. With good leaders, it is possible to effectuate conditions for effective and mutually beneficial cooperation on national levels.

But Israel is concerned with the short-term. Israel's policy reflects the perception that a colonialist oppression is the way to go and one of the ways to maintain effective colonialist control is to regulate the leadership of the oppressed people.

In the global community, especially with the internet, such oppressive controls do not necessarily effectuate expected results.

Young Palestinians have proven that they can find their way out of the lack of well-funded university education. Many Palestinians are found in Ph.D. programs of some of the world's most elite universities.

In fact, Palestinians have done so well on the international scene in advancing despite the difficulties and the hardships, that they are perceived by many to be the most intellectual Arabs.

It is, in fact, not surprising to find Palestinians playing important roles in the Arab world. Often, computer experts and infrastructure builders in the Arab world tend to be Palestinian. In Jordan, where almost 50% of the population is Palestinian, it is not surprising to see the important roles that Palestinians have played in building of Jordan as a modern state with great future potential, economically and politically.

Palestinians have found ways to find educational opportunities in Arab and non-Arab nations. Many Palestinian Catholics have benefited from the positive support of the Roman Catholic Church.

Protestants in America have particularly taken issue with the oppression of Palestinians and some of the mainline denominations have taken great incentives to train the brightest among Palestinians.

Yale Divinity School in Connecticut and Graduate Theological Union in California have particularly raised awareness of Palestinian issues in the past. More recently, Fuller Theological Seminary in California and Westminster Theological

Seminary in Pennsylvania have taken up issues relating to the oppression in the Middle East context.

There are now independent evangelical Christian groups specifically working toward helping Palestinians. Many of these organizations seek to provide scholarships to capable Palestinian students who have, in essence, no support from the State of Israel and otherwise may not have the opportunity to gain the necessary education to reach their full potential.

Due to the counter-attack by American and other Western European Christians of Israeli deprivation of educational opportunities for Palestinians, Palestinians have been able to advance their pool of brain power.

American and Western European help of Palestinians has not been only in getting capable Palestinians out of the Occupied Territories for a good education in the West.

American and Western European Christians have sent in capable teachers and professors into the Occupied Territories to help train Palestinians where they live.

A good example of this is with the American operated The Albright Institute in Jerusalem. The Albright Institute is dedicated primarily to the study of the Bible and archaeology relating to the Bible. There is a permanent staff, and every year top researchers stay in the institute for a period of three months to a whole year.

Some of the scholars at The Albright Institute frequently go and teach in Palestinian universities. Often, it is a good will gesture more than anything else, but many Biblical scholars are willing to go meet and talk with Palestinian students.

Not only do Palestinian students gain the opportunity to interact with top scholars from around the world, sometimes educational relations are forged that allow them to further their studies or benefit academically in other ways.

It does not hurt that many Biblical scholars feel a sense of Christian duty to the oppressed. Many of them, therefore, see teaching in Palestinian universities or giving special lectures there as a way to live in practical living ethics they hold to be dear.

The fact that The Albright Institute is in East Jerusalem also helps to facilitate a positive relationship between the American academic institute and Palestinian universities.

The Albright Institute has historically had a positive relationship with Palestinians. As many Palestinian Christians are in the near proximity, Bible scholars sometimes befriend Palestinian Christians in the area in the context of a church fellowship.

Given the fact that the global community is getting smaller and smaller every year, it is impossible for the State of Israel to maintain an oppressive control over the Palestinians. "Keeping people down policy" in the area of education clearly shows that there are more than two parties involved and others are happily willing to lend their support to the oppressed.

The Israeli oppression of Palestinians is not confined to university levels. Israel has proven that it tries to practice "Keeping people down policy" on high school levels as well.

Like universities in the Occupied Territories, secondary education is grossly underfunded. But besides the lack of available funds, the State of Israel has proven again and again that it does all it can to discourage developing the Palestinian secondary education program both in terms of quality and in terms of size.

The Roman Catholic Church has sought to create Catholic schools from kindergarten to high school, but often they are barred from building constructions because they are simply denied building permits. There may be excuses given but they are flimsy at best in most cases.

And in cases where building permits are granted, Catholic Church officials often are hassled and the permits delayed. Such measures may have the intention of demoralization and discouragement.

In many cases, Catholic Church leaders have been able to wade through Israeli oppression effectively and provide venues for good education. But with more tolerance and support on the part of Israeli government, more can be done to educate Palestinian young and give them a fair chance at life.

You can see why I hate Israel. Israel is an unethical oppressor. Israel deprives the Palestinians of what is rightfully theirs. A good education and a shot at a bright future should be the property of every Palestinian. However, the State of Israel has proven again and again that it wants to play the Evil One.

The State of Israel is so bent on oppressing the Palestinians that their policies have harassed the Christian Church and its leaders from around the world. As a secular Hindu, I cannot in good conscience speak favourably at all about the Jewish State that is an embodiment of evil in today's world.

Denial

Denial is a painful thing. Perhaps, there is nothing more painful than being denied by the person from whom you want recognition. All forms of denial are painful, although some forms of denial may be more painful than others. Denial can be seen as a category of human suffering.

What the Palestinians experience in the Occupied Territories is denial, plain and simple. They have been denied for a long time. Years and years have they experienced denial. Denial is not something that just started this year.

What are Palestinians denied? Palestinians are denied their state. Palestinians are not allowed their independence. They are not allowed a nation to call their own. In essence, Palestinians are denied their right to self-determination as a people.

What must certainly be very painful for Palestinians is the fact that they are denied by Israelis. There are several reasons why the fact that Israelis are those who deny is particularly painful.

First of all, Israel is the Jewish nation, and Palestinians have treated Jews with respect and kindness when the Jews were the minority in Palestine. Yep, that's what it is.

It is easy to forget that the State of Israel is only a little over 50 years old. And it's not like a form of an Israeli nation existed before then in the region in recent history.

To put it into perspective, we can see the example of China. Currently, China is a Communist state (although people can argue that it is a type of benign Communism or a capitalist Communism). But before the reality of the Communist state, China existed as a country with another form of government. In fact, China existed as a nation (or kingdom) for thousands of years.

Same people lived in the area. Many people in China can trace their ancestry back hundreds of years. And those who do not have specific records can be reasonably sure that their ancestry goes back hundreds, if not thousands of years, in the general region of China. Even if technically, there is a different form of government, there had been the most important element of the country, namely the Chinese populace.

The State of Israel cannot claim this. The modern secular state of Israel was created little over 50 years ago, and the people who came to rule and live as citizens were not native to the region. Many of the Jews who came to set up the Jewish state were Jews who have lived in Europe for hundreds, if not thousands, of years.

In other words, most of the Jews who came to Israel to form the Jewish state were foreigners to the area. Before they came, the land had been lived in by Palestinians for thousands of years.

74

If the measure of ownership is by how long a people lived in a region, the Palestinians win by a long shot.

Palestinians have lived in the region. Palestinians have tilled the land. Palestinians have experienced fortunes and terrors attached to the land of Palestine.

European Jews who came to set up the Jewish State did not really have entitlement to the land, except for the fact that they were allowed to colonize the land in the Zionist project with the approval of the British Empire.

Before the founding of the State of Israel, most of the people who lived in the region were Palestinians.

But there were Jews living in the area, particularly in Galilee, although there were not many of them.

One thing is clear. In the thousands of years that the majority of Jews lived outside of Palestine (Israel), the minority of Jews who settled in Palestine were treated kindly by the Palestinians.

After centuries of Palestinian kindness, Jews from Europe refused to return the favor and show kindness to Palestinians. The Jewish denial of the Palestinian State is an extension of the painful denial.

To understand the historical reality better, perhaps it is helpful to rehash the history.

In 70 AD, the Roman Empire used its heavy hand on the Jews and kicked every single Jew out of Jerusalem. The Jerusalem Temple was completely destroyed, and Jews were forced out of the city.

The land was spattered with salt so that it would become unsuitable for farming. Romans wanted to ensure that Jews will not return to Jerusalem, and those who return will not have food to eat. It was a cruel policy of expulsion.

Since 70 AD, no Jew really returned to Jerusalem (certainly, not in significant numbers). That is not to say that Jews could not have returned to Jerusalem.

After the fall of the Pagan Roman Empire, Jews could have returned to Jerusalem and set up Jewish communities there. There were enough wealthy Jews in the Diaspora that it was probably possible for Jews to rebuild the Jerusalem Temple.

However, this did not happen. Jews decided to stay away from Jerusalem. There are several reasons for this.

Jews stayed away from Jerusalem because many of them have made Diaspora their home. It was much more comfortable for them to live in the Diaspora with their family, relatives, and friends close by. There were many active Jewish communities in the Diaspora, so Jews felt that they had all they needed in the Diaspora to be happy and to be Jews.

Secondly, Jews stayed away from Jerusalem because returning to Jerusalem meant that they had to rebuilt from scratch.

Since Jews have been away from Jerusalem for centuries when they were allowed to return to Jerusalem, they did not know what to expect. Many probably felt the project undaunting and perhaps impossible to accomplish. There were too many logistic problems to consider, and many Jews refused to go the distance.

But more importantly, Jews stayed away from Jerusalem because Rabbinic Judaism had a vested interest in not reviving a Temple-based Judaism. This third point must be emphasized.

Despite all the logistic problems and the comforts of the Diaspora, if the Jewish communal leaders strongly urged, there probably would have been massive returns to Jerusalem. It was certainly not out of the realm of possibility to construct a glorious Jerusalem and rebuilt the Temple, if the Jewish communities in the Diaspora had the incentive.

The problem is that rabbis did not want that. Rabbis were happy with a Talmud (text) based Judaism that flourished after the destruction of the Jerusalem Temple. To rebuilt the Temple and bring back the authority of the priests meant that the rabbis would lose out.

So, you can say that Jewish rabbis, in fact, were selfish and discouraged the return of Jews to Jerusalem. Thus, for nearly 2000 years, Jews stayed away, not because they had to, but because that was the spirit of Jewish communities, encouraged by the rabbis and other Jewish communal leaders.

Without going into too much detail, it is easy to see that there was a fundamental difference between a priest (hereditary) leadership based on the Jerusalem Temple with a sacrificial system and a legal leadership based on religious texts that denigrated hereditary leadership and elevated a type of educational elitism.

Educational elites felt they had a vested interest in depriving hereditary peers of their authority structure. Return to Jerusalem would have given them *de facto* power.

In light of the voluntary refusal of European Jews to return to Jerusalem, their ethical claim to the land seems specious at best.

Palestinians who know the history are rightly peeved that European Jews used colonialism to get into Palestine and claim the land as their own. What irks Palestinians more is that Jews seem to try to claim an ethical entitlement to the land.

Anyone who knows the history can appreciate the disgust that some Palestinians may feel at such hypocrisy, particularly among rabbinic leaders.

But ever since the founding of the State of Israel a little over 50 years ago, Jews have used specious arguments to prop up

Jewish entitlement to the land and exclude the Palestinians from their own land.

The fact is that Palestinians are willing to share land, and that is why the Jewish denial of the Palestinian state feels more unjust. Palestinians are willing to share the land that they lived on for thousands of years, but the Jews are not?

Palestinians are actually being magnanimous, and Jews are being stingy. There is ample land to go around between the two peoples, and there can be two nations friendly side by side.

Besides the pain of denial contrasted with Palestinian magnanimity, the Palestinians feel the pain of denial in light of the understanding of who those who deny are.

Palestinians are denied the right to their own nation by Jews. It is common knowledge that Jews have struggled for a nation to call their own. The whole phenomenon in history is called Zionism.

And there are writings after writings about Zionism. Zionists have written prodigious amount of literature. A visit to the local library will prove this point.

Even now, there are Zionist writings. There is writing after writing about the importance of Jewish nationalism. A visit to the Hillel House of a local university will convince you that the Zionist discourse is alive and well in modern America.

And this is certainly the case in the State of Israel. There is a lot of Zionist writings. You can find in both Hebrew and English writings by Israeli thinkers on Jewish nationalism and self-determination.

Given the prodigious writing on the issue of the fundamental right of a people to self-determination and nationhood, the Jewish denial of the Palestinian State seems particularly unfair and hypocritical.

If anybody in the world should understand the Palestinian right to the Palestinian State, it should be the Jews. Look at all that they have written.

Ironically, however, it is the Jews who are the most vociferous against the Palestinian state.

You can see why I hate Israel. You can understand why many people in the world hate Israel.

If there were not so much writing on the concept of self-determination, freedom, nationhood, maybe it would be different. But given the facts of the situation, Jews are inviting hatred.

It almost feels like it would be wrong not to hate Israel, given what they are doing to the Palestinians. Even the most magnanimous individual in the world will find it difficult to respect or like Israel under the circumstances.

Given that third party individuals will feel indignation at Israel's unfair denial of the Palestinian state, you can understand, to a certain extent, why the Palestinians may be very, very angry at the whole thing. Yep, that's what it is.

Besides the angering element of Israeli hypocrisy in denying Palestinians their right to self-determination and nationhood, I find another irritating element in the whole issue of denial.

I see in the State of Israel a fundamental denial of the individual. The individual, whether he is Palestinian, Jewish, or Indian, should be respected as a rationale being.

The Enlightenment showed humanity the beauty of the human mind and the human potential. The Enlightenment emphasized the need to respect human beings as individuals. Perhaps, this is the best gift from the movement to humanity. No longer should we objectify the other, but treat the other with respect as individual human beings.

The State of Israel refuses to see Palestinians as individuals worthy of respect. Israelis have created a culture that perceives the Palestinians as a homogenized Other. All individuality of the Palestinians are subsumed under the negative generalities of Otherness.

To me, that is simply disgusting. Have not the Jews learned from their own experience?

In my opinion, the way that Israelis are behaving gives the moral right to others to treat the Jews the same way, as a negative homogenized whole.

Whereas people's perception of Jews are not legislated in most cases, Jewish perception of Palestinians finds legislation in the policies of the Jewish state.

This is what I find particularly disgusting. Not only are Palestinians not respected as individuals, who should be given respect because they are rational beings, the State of Israel has the gall to dehumanize them legally through policies that homogenize them.

A good example is the liberal policy on search and seizure. The Israeli Defence Force (IDF) seems to have unbridled power in its right to search and arrest Palestinians at will. There is legal support as well as the practical infrastructure to allow the IDF to do this.

The rationale behind this is simple. The State of Israel expects the Palestinians to be potential terrorists. In essence, all Palestinians are homogenized into the idea of "the Palestinian terrorist."

This objectification and homogenization generate and maintain the Otherness of Palestinians. It is the denial of the individual. It represents a fundamental disrespect for the human person. In essence, the Israeli objectification of and disrespect for the Palestinian individual is an affront to humanity.

It is no surprise that the International Court on Human Rights wanted to try Israeli Prime Minister Ariel Sharon for Crimes against Humanity. Sharon has shown again and again a fundamental disrespect for the individual and for human rights. And in many ways, he mirrors the sentiment of many in Israel, unfortunately.

Although it would be difficult to fault every Israeli, it is possible to fault the State of Israel, based on its policies.

Israeli policies have been one of denial – denial of the individual. And for this, I find it easy to hate Israel.

I do hope that the State of Israel will change their course. I would like to give Israel the benefit of the doubt. However, I am also realistic. I know what Israel has done. And until Israel changes its course of action, I feel completely justified in my righteous hatred of Israel.

The Bully Factor

I am sorry but I will not apologize for my hatred of Israel. I know that Hinduism prohibits such a passionate hatred, but I feel justified in my stance. First of all, I am a secular Hindu, so I do not subscribe to all the religious commands of Hinduism.

Secondly, I believe that hatred of injustice and oppression is taking an ethical stance for righteousness. In fact, I would go as far as to argue that if I do not hate Israel for its oppression, then I would be participating in Israel's evil.

Empathetic hatred of oppression – siding with the oppressed – is an active form of non-violent resistance. At this point, I, as a secular Hindu, have emphasized no violent action, but a personal commitment of condemnation against Israeli oppression. My hatred of Israel, therefore, forms a pacific resistance of evil on a moral level.

Thirdly, Hinduism emphasizes *karma*. Israel's oppression is bad *karma* that is an evil force in the world. Israel's evil *karma* can fuel global imbalance and chaos. Active opposition to this evil *karma* is needed. My personal participation to balance global peace is to engage in personal hatred of Israel on the level of sentiment. The very fact that I hate Israel will balance the evil *karma* created by Israeli oppression. If my proactive, personal *karma* can turn the tide of global collapse and contribute to global positivity, then I am happy to do so.

I speak as a secular Hindu, but I can speak as an enlightened European as well. Hegel's philosophy clearly emphasizes a result guided by two opposing forces. When a thesis exists, an antithesis can balance the thesis, resulting in a synthesis. There is much to be said for this Heidelberg School of thought.

Since the thesis is the evil of the Israeli oppression, at least I can provide on a discussion level a proper antithesis to bring a synthesis that will be equitable. Of course, I understand the limitations of describing things on the discourse level. Hegelian philosophy was more concerned with actions and actual societal forces. Despite what can be termed as a revised Hegelian discourse on my part, I feel my arguments can properly be termed "a Hegelian solution."

Especially with the existence of human rights laws and international institutions, a Hegelian type solution on a discourse level must be given more weight than it is today. The alternative is an actual (action-oriented) Hegelian conclusion on a societal level with deep changes. And as most Hegelian thinkers posit, forces cannot be controlled, and often they result in dire consequences for those involved as well as bystanders.

In light of the tragic forecast of most Hegelians on societal issues where powerful (often uncontrollable) forces are at play, my proposition on a discourse level provides a viable and positive solution that can help all sides. My counter-action, or antithesis, in essence, will help Israelis in the long-run, ironically enough. For, it is my very discourse, providing the synthesis on a discourse level (and not at an action level!) that may find an amenable synthesis on a discourse level (and not at an action level!).

Of course, I recognize the fact that the realm of discourse and the realm of action are not always completely separate. They often interact and even develop cause-and-effect relationships.

Even so, I feel morally justified in my hatred of injustice and oppression by the State of Israel. I feel so strongly in my moral right (and obligation) to hate the injustice and oppression of Israel that even if there were harm to result on Israel on an action level (in Hegelian dialectal terms), I would feel exonerated.

Sometimes, resisting evil requires violence. You cannot free a hostage without killing off some of the oppressors who put him in captivity. Murders of such oppress-ors would be completely justified on any ethical level. If Israelis are killed as the direct result of my discourse and someone could prove the direct link (which is impossible, obviously), I would feel no fault morally or ethically.

The facts are clear. The moral and ethical fault lies with the Israelis. The evidence is present in the court of public opinion. Israelis are oppressing the Palestinians. International courts have already ruled more than a few times regarding Israel's culpability. Israel refuses to change course. Israel is clearly deserving of punishment in International Law terms. Currently, there are no international legal (or human rights) organizations capable of seeking restitution for the wrongs committed by the State of Israel, but that does not deny Israel's fundamental culpability. Israel is at fault, so they owe restitution.

Thus, if the restitution comes in some form of active *karma*, and if my writing contributes to the rightening of the wrongs, I will take pride in it. United Nations is on my side. International community opinion is on my side. International human rights laws are on my side.

Several of Israel's major human rights violations and oppressive measures have been outlined in this book. And I would like to add to the evidence by citing another category of wrongs committed by the State of Israel.

I am calling it, "The Bully Factor." The State of Israel is a big bully. There is no question about it. Israel's bully identity can be seen on the discourse as well as action levels. Yep, that's what it is.

On the level of discourse, Israel is always making itself out to be the greatest military power in the region. Israelis often boast of having the strongest army in the region. And I would not be surprised if you heard from an Israeli that the Israeli Air Force is the best in the world. It is certainly a part of the popular Israeli discourse. And more than a few Israeli experts have expressed this popular notion on a public level.

The reasons for the pride in the Israeli Air Force are easy to identify. Israeli Air Force has some of the most advanced military airplanes in the world. During the Cold War, Americans identified Israel as a type of a satellite buffer state against Eastern European invasion of Western Europe and the United States.

As a result, Americans trained and provided sophisticated Air Force equipment. Even though after the fall of Eastern Europe, America started to pull its support out of Israel and its military program, the fact that the fall of the Iron Curtain is a fairly recent event has played a part in not providing an accurate picture of the American pull of support. Furthermore, the planes in the Israeli arsenal provided in the past are still quite advanced by any standards.

Another reason why Israel has confidence in its Air Force is because they have played crucial roles in winning wars for Israel. In most of the wars that Israel fought with its Arab neighbors, the deciding (advantage) factor was the Air Force. It should be noted, however, that this pride may be misplaced.

Had Arab nations had comparatively advanced aircrafts, the outcome might have been different. As mentioned, America had provided Israel with superior aircraft because America used Israel as a station of warning and a possible first line of defence in the event of a Cold War developing into an actual war.

Yet, I recognize the fact that the Israeli Air Force has played an important role in its military victories in the past.

There is yet another reason why Israelis take pride in their Air Force. Even in times of peace, the Israeli Air Force engaged in highly dangerous and successful operations. The most prominent of the operations carried out by the Israeli Air Force was the bombing of nuclear facilities in Iraq. Israel flew over enemy airspace and effectively wiped out nuclear power plants.

Yet, it may be important to emphasize here that times are changing. Iran has nuclear installations, and Iran pre-emptively warned Israel not to do what it did to Iraq. Israel has complied with Iran's warnings and has not attempted to attack the nuclear installations.

The reason why Israel is obeying Iran's demands can be seen in various factors. First, the United States has steadily decreased its support of Israel since the fall of the Iron Curtain. Today, Israel cannot be confident at all that America will come to its aid in the event such an action may initiate a war.

America is not bound by any treaty to help Israel in its offensive start of war. Bombing nuclear sites in Iran would constitute aggressive behavior, which will most likely bring about the condemnation by the United States. Some Jews fear that such an incident will give the Republican-controlled Congress the excuse to sever all ties with the Jewish State in the name of American national interest (especially in lieu of America's War on Terrorism, which Israeli action would aggravate).

Secondly, Iran today is not Iraq yesterday. It is possible that Iran already has biological, chemical, and nuclear weapons. If Israel attacked after an explicit public warning, by the rules of warfare, Iran will be allowed to retaliate against Israeli act of war by emptying their weapons on Israeli soil. It would take 30 minutes to completely wipe out all of Israel. Israel genuinely fears the possibility of such a warfare and its consequences.

Thirdly, Israel has lost the respect of the international community, and Israeli leaders know this. The State of Israel is not perceived as a peaceful nation or a peace-loving nation. There will be no sympathy for an act of aggression.

In fact, Israel knows too well that there are many nations in the world, which would be very happy to condemn Israel openly and impose crippling economic and political sanctions. In light of the trouble with terrorism, most nations will have their hands forced to condemn Israel with actual sanctions, were Israel to engage in any form of aggression that could be destabilizing globally. Most nations have their own interests to protect and will care less about the Jewish State.

Thus, it is important to recognize that while there are historical reasons why the Israeli Air Force has gained the reputation that it did, current situations make past events and credits absolutely nugatory. Past accomplishments do not mean anything in light of today's global environment.

What should concern Israelis particularly, however, is the image of Israel as a bully. What seemed to be an image that the global community could ignore (or even praise) is now turning out to be disadvantageous particularly for America and Western Europe, which are struggling to hold their society together. Israel is certainly seen as a liability. This perception is most clear in the way Washington DC is distancing itself from Israel, more and more.

The problem is that the State of Israel seems to be ignoring the sensitive situation of America and Western Europe. Israel continues to engage in bully tactics vis-à-vis the Arab neighbors, and, more importantly, against Palestinians.

Israel still does not understand that the 21st Century is completely different from the last century.

Yep, that's what it is. Israel is still living in the past.

I have one word for Israel: "oil." Oil is becoming more and more important around the world. And in the absence of the Cold War, there is no conflict of interest to hinder America or Western European nations from embracing oil-rich Arab nations.

Americans and Europeans know that oil is crucial. In fact, America and Western Europe will collapse if Arab nations withheld oil for several weeks.

Think about all the things that require oil. Energy is driven by oil. And Arab nations have the oil that is needed to fuel energy in households, businesses, and global transportation.

In fact, without oil, the world's most powerful military will not be able to operate. It will be like an advanced computer system that is lacking software. It's absolutely useless.

No matter how advanced the technology, currently oil is needed to fuel the energy. Oil is the most precious thing in the world today.

Without oil, people will drop dead quickly from all kinds of disasters. Oil is as important as oxygen in America and Western Europe.

And oil is becoming more and more important with growing technologization of the society. And this trend is spreading across the globe.

Arab nations have the oil, so the world is dependent on it. You can call it luck. You can call it God's blessing. Call it what you want, but the Arabs have it.

By the virtue of the fact that Arab nations have what is absolutely necessary in today's world, Arab nations have the ready ears of world's nations, even if they do not visibly show it.

In fact, if the Arab nations wanted to, they could collude and control oil prices during election time. If they do it effect-ively, they could most likely get the president they want elected in America.

Arab nations hold tremendous amount of actual and potential power in global matters.

And Arab nations have diversified. Arab nations today are not Arab nations yesterday. Elite Arabs today are not elite

Arabs yesterday. Many of the elite Arabs are Oxford, Cambridge, Harvard, Stanford educated. They are bright. They know how to use their wealth to create more wealth. And they have many friends in the West.

It is no surprise that Arab individuals in Arab countries have taken a large stake in American financial sectors. There are many Arabs actively involved in trade and in the American stock market. And there is more and more branching out into sectors that are important even domestically in the context of America and Western Europe.

Arab nations and Arab individuals cannot just be brushed aside like they could several decades ago. Israel has to realize that their image of Arabs as a backward, ignorant people is certainly outdated (if it were even true in the first place, which is very doubtful).

What this means in the international scene is that Israel can expect America and Western Europe to uphold Arab interests over Israel's. Israel really has nothing to offer to America and Western Europe, since the Iron Curtain fell tumbling down.

Simply put, America no longer needs Israel. The same is true for Western Europe. As painful as this may be to accept, particularly for the old guard, it is true. Sooner Israelis accept this reality, the better they will be to wade through the minefields created by the vacuum after the fall of the Iron Curtain.

Arab nations currently hold all the cards. As long as oil is the primary source of energy, Arab nations have the potential to dictate global discourse and direction.

Granted, Arab nations have not effectively utilized their potential power. The question remains if they are interested in global domination. All the indicators are there that Arab nations have no interest in global domination. There really isn't any expansionist Arab regime at the present. All indicators are there that most Arab nations desire to remain peaceful as long as their values are respected and their religious sites not desecrated.

Given these indicators, Arab nations easily endear themselves to America and to Western Europe, particularly in today's pluralistic, politically correct environment.

In fact, the movie, *Fahrenheit 911* showed clearly that America's elites are bending over backwards to please Arab elites in the most elite settings in America. Arab nations not only have oil but they have the financial capital that American businesses want.

Israel cannot honestly think that America and American businesses will ignore their essential needs of energy and financial opportunities available in the Arab world for Jewish interests in the Jewish State?

To assume that America and Americans have a vested interest in the Jewish State would be at best fooling themselves. Israel must recognize the fact that most Americans actually do not like Israel. Here is the evidence:

First of all, let's not forget the historical hatred of Jews. A fact is a fact, and denying it will not help in any way. There has been anti-Semitism in Western History even before the birth of Jesus Christ. There were anti-Semitic writings by Roman historians. There is ample evidence that ancient Romans, who are considered Pagans by the Christian Church, persecuted Jews.

Reasons given by the Romans are that Jews were too cliquish and tried to emphasize Jewish distinctives in an offensive manner.

Of course, you can make a moral judgement of the Romans and say that they were wrong. But it does not change history. In the history of Western civilization, ancient Romans have practiced active forms of hatred of Jews.

It was not only under the Pagan empire that the Jews were reviled and hated. The Holy Bible accuses the Jews of colluding to have Jesus Christ crucified and actually having him killed. And as long as the Holy Bible is the standard of the Christian Church, this understanding will not change.

The fact that there were bitter conflicts between Jews and Christians in the first few centuries does not help matters in the perception that Jews and Christians are enemies.

The Book of Acts in the Bible chronicles a violent conflict between Jews and Christians. In fact, the Book of Acts gives a portrayal of Jewish synagogue leaders hiring mercenaries and other secretive agents to persecute Christians.

The Book of Galatians portrays a conflict between Jews and Christians. St. Paul accuses Christians of Jewish origin of trying to subvert Christianity from within.

The picture that the Holy Bible gives is clearly one of bitter conflict between Jews and Christians.

But it's not just the Holy Bible that provides a picture of active animosity between Jews and Christians. Early Christian writings, such as Justin Martyr's *Dialogue with Trypho the Jew*, clearly indicates an on-going conflict well past the time of St. Paul the Apostle.

In fact, many of the Christian Church Fathers from the first three centuries of Christian history clearly exhibit an active conflict with Jews.

But it is not only Christian documents that evidence conflict between Jews and Christians. Jewish documents clearly indicate a vociferous conflict.

In fact, *The Eighteen Benedictions* has a section that makes it mandatory for synagogues to kick out Jews who convert to Christianity from the synagogue.

It is important that synagogues in the ancient world were not like synagogues in today's America. In today's America, synagogues are not central for a typical American Jew's life. It may be more important than other aspects of his life, but it is certainly only one of his many social associations.

In the ancient world, it wasn't that way. The synagogue, in essence, was the primary (or even the only) social association for a Jew. To be kicked out of the synagogue meant that he lost his social setting.

To put this more clearly into focus, if a Jew converted to Christianity but wanted to remain socially in contact with his family, it was often done through the synagogue. To be expelled from the synagogue meant, in essence, being forced out of your family. In essence, your family, by the virtue of their association in the synagogue, could not associate with you any longer.

Thus, converting to Christianity brought you under the curse of *The Eighteen Benedictions*. You effectively became an Untouchable.

The Jewish conflict with Christians in the ancient world is clearly documented. However, the conflict was not only confined to the ancient period. In fact, there are ample Jewish writings from the Middle Ages of the conflict between Jews and Christians. Perhaps, it may not be inaccurate to say that there are more explicitly anti-Christian writings in Jewish circles than the other way around.

The picture is clear. All throughout European history, Christianity and Judaism stood in opposition. The hostility went both ways.

Often, hostilities climaxed and ended up in violence. Given that there is a greater number of Christians in society (or rather, there are more non-Jews in society) in most settings, Jews generally ended up suffering greatly at the end.

Jews were expelled from England and Spain in prominent historical incidences. There were violent murders of Jews in Russia and Germany. There were many less prominent cases of violence against Jews all over Europe.

Sometimes, the violence against Jews was spontaneous and initiated by the working classes. Other times, there were specific anti-Jewish laws passed by the government to persecute the Jews.

The conflict between Christians and Jews can be seen as a defining characteristic of over 2000 years of European history. Perhaps, it may not be wrong to speak of an internalization (or even automation) of the conflict. More than a few Jewish writers have written about the internalization of anti-Semitism in the subconscience of everyone of European descent.

If they are correct and if history is of any value for understanding the present, then the only logical conclusion is that Jews are not particularly liked in America or Western Europe.

Put in another way, it's probably not wise to bet your life that Americans and Europeans love Jews, given the historical precedents.

Besides the fact that Jews are probably disliked generally in America and Western Europe, there is another reason why it is safe to assume that Americans generally do not like Israel. America is becoming more and more Christian with each passing day. And the most popular version of Christian understanding of the end of times encourages a Christian Jerusalem.

The fact that Israel is a Jewish State and that Jerusalem is discoursed in Israel as a Jewish capital does not endear Israel to the Christians in America. Americans want a Christian Jerusalem.

For evidence, Jews only have to turn their ears to the language of "New Jerusalem" or "True Israel." Christian eschatology envisions a Christian Jerusalem with Jesus Christ as the head.

Some even talk about the need of Jerusalem to be the capital of the Kingdom of Christ. Thus, it is no surprise that many Baptist Christians go to Israel and go first to the Church of Holy Sepulcre to see the place where Jesus was killed (with Jews as understood to being the Christ-killers).

It is probably accurate to assume that a desire for a Christian Jerusalem is partly behind the drive to convert every Jew in America. Several evangelical Christian groups, including the largest Christian block, the Southern Baptists, have taken oath to try to convert every single Jew to Christianity.

It is important for Israel to recognize the fact that Christians in America envisions a True Israel – namely, a Christian Israel with Christ as the king.

There is yet another reason why Americans tend to dislike Israel. Israel rubs America the wrong way in the way it seems to colonize the Palestinians.

Perhaps, it is important to acknow- ledge how the United States became a nation. It was a colony of England, and it engaged in a freedom fight to become free. There are slogans like, "Live free or die!" There is no question that freedom is one of the most important values for Americans.

Particularly with leftist Americans, Israel's refusal to grant Palestinians free- dom is a sore point. Many Americans resent Israel's reluctance to grant Palestinians a state of their own and see it in terms of the experience of the United States before the American Revolutionary War.

Given that July 4th is such an important holiday in America and given the fact that the American Revolutionary War is taught in every school, Israelis should not be surprised by the hostilities that many Americans hold against Israel, that more and more Americans perceive as colonialist oppressor.

Certainly, it would be a mistake to assume that America supports Israel. This might have been functionally true during the Cold War in the last century, but such an assumption can be very costly in this century.

Coupled with the fact that America is pro-Arab, at least functionally due to need for oil and financial capital, Israel should plan accordingly to survive this century.

Unfortunately, the bullying tactics that characterized the State of Israel in the last century does not seem to be abating. Israel still seems to think that this is the 20th century.

The clearest indicators are found in two sectors. First, Israel is still playing bully against its neighbors. Instead of working with its neighbors, particularly Jordan and Egypt, for mutual cooperation and development, the State of Israel operates as if these two nations are just a little better than enemies.

There is the tacit understanding that Israel may go to war with either Egypt or Jordan. There is almost a foreboding expectation – a self-fulfilling prophecy, if you will – that a war might break out and that these two Arab nations will attack Israel.

Of course, everything is possible. Aliens can land on Jerusalem and proclaim the supreme Martian rule in Israel. But the likelihood is small.

Israel should work to minimize dangerous possibilities through friendship building and mutual cooperation. So far, Israel seems to be averting such a positive course of action.

Instead, the State of Israel remains aloof and seems to send out threatening signals to its neighborhood countries of Egypt and Jordan.

Instead of threatening with the proclamation of the possession of nuclear weapons and a great Air Force, Israel can take a step of being a friend. For instance, if Israel engaged in joint military exercises frequently, it is a way to show a friendship stance.

It's not like Israel has to divulge its military secrets. It can engage in a superficial level military cooperation and joint exercises. The point is that such a gesture will be a move away from a hostile, bully stance that it has taken.

Secondly, Israel has proven itself to be a bully in trying to connect groups that it has accused of being terrorists with what is generally seen as global terrorism. It is like trying to find more excuses to bash in those whom Israel identifies as terrorists.

For instance, Israel has used the Global War on Terror, announced by the United States, to kill off leaders of political organizations that it considers terrorists. There are several problems with this.

First of all, the whole world does not necessarily consider the organizations that Israel considers terrorist as terrorist organizations. This holds true certainly among Muslim nations, like Malaysia, as well as among Western European nations. So, it's no surprise that past several killings of supposed terrorists leaders have been condemned around the world.

It is important to recognize that even most Muslim countries consider Al-Qaida, blamed for September 11th attacks in New York and Washington DC, as terrorist. However, this is not true with many of the people whom the State of Israel consider terrorist.

The State of Israel has been seen as liberal in applying the term terrorist. Thus, sometimes, Muslim religious leaders have been inaccurately identified as terrorists.

If Christians applied such a liberal application of terrorism, then there will be many Jewish rabbis in America who may find trouble with the law.

Secondly, many in America and Western Europe resent what they see as Israel's opportunism at the tragedy of global terrorism. When Israel bends backwards and forwards to try to tie those whom Israel identifies as its terrorists and globally agreed world terrorists, people resent what they perceive as Israel trying to steal the spotlight. It appears like Israel is begging for attention.

People feel disgusted when they see Israel trying to portray itself as a victim. Perhaps, it will help Israel if Israel saw things from the other side of the fence.

Prime Minister Itzak Rabin and Palestinian Authority President Yassir Arafat met to forge peace and found the Palestinian State. It was perceived as a historic event. Both of the leaders were given the Nobel Peace Prize for the initiated peace process. The whole world cheered in optimism at the Peace in the Middle East that would lead to Global Peace. Businesses started to flow in and invest in Israel in a new show of optimism.

The Israeli Prime Minster was shot to death by an Orthodox Jewish law student at Bar Ilan University in Tel Aviv, Israel. And the peace process was summarily dismissed. The whole world wept for Prime Minister Rabin, and when the grieving was done, they whole world became disgusted at the course of action that Israel followed, which seem to desecrate Rabin's memory.

Many felt like they were made fools of by the Israelis and came to have deep-seated resentment against Israelis. After all the fan fair, all the press, the Nobel Peace Prize, how dare they pull this one on us? Israel made us look like fools!

The impact of the rising grudge is yet to be felt in real terms, but it is safe to assume that it will have dire, negative repercussions for Israel and the Jews. Resentment is a scary thing, and history has shown what can happen as a result.

It is about time that the State of Israel stops playing the bully and try to see a more constructive end to their hostilities. The whole world is watching, and, frankly, we are not impressed in the least bit.

Rising resentment will give expression somehow and if history is any indicator, Jews will lose out. So, before things get out of hand, it would be wise for Israel to turn their course of aggression. This is one chicken-fight Israel will certainly lose.

But Israel doesn't seem to be turning in the constructive direction. Israel is continuing to be the bully.

And this is why I hate Israel. Israel has always been a bully since the founding of the State of Israel over 50 years ago and it's continuing to be a bully. And I presume

Israel will continue to be a bully until its utter destruction.

I hate bullies. I always have. And that is one of the primary reasons why I hate Israel.

Maybe Israel will surprise me, but I doubt it.

Conclusion

I hate Israel with every righteous fiber in my being. The State of Israel has a racist ideology in Zionism, happily played the role of modern colonialist oppressor, and bullied the Middle East. Israel represents all that is evil in the world, today. All freedom-loving individuals with a sense of human rights and social justice are ethically obliged to hate the oppression and injustice that Israel perpetuates and executes.

I have outlined many reasons and given ample evidence for why Israel should be hated by every self-respecting citizen of the world. I can, at this point, encourage you, the reader, to join me in the righteous hatred of Israel.

Through the positive, counter *karma* creation in collective hatred of Israeli oppression, we all do our part for the good of humanity. Global peace has to start somewhere, and active hatred of Israel's oppressive policies is a good place to start.

About the Author

Priya Gandhi-Ganesh considers herself a secular Hindu and very concerned with social justice and human rights. She has taught in India and other parts of the world.